# When Your
# HEART
## Says
## "It's Your Time To Soar!"

David Chametzky

Copyright © 2022 by David Chametzky

ISBN: 978-1-64810-214-1

All rights reserved. No part of this book may be reproduced mechanically, electronically, virtually, or by any other means, including photocopying without written permission of the publisher. It is illegal to copy this book, post it to any website or distribute it by any other means without permission from the publisher.

Published by Perfect Publishing Co.

This book is dedicated to your heart,
and to the chambers of my heart.

# THESE PICTURES

These pictures were gifts from each of my daughters —
one special Father's day!

# TABLE OF CONTENTS

Section One – HEARTBEATS.................... Page 1

Section Two – GOOD PATHWAYS ............... Page 23

Section Three – TRUE FLIGHTS ................. Page 53

# THIS BOOK

This book shares stories and poems curated through the life of the author and pathfinder, David Chametzky. We all walk along various paths in our lives and meet people who share their hearts. Our hearts always guide us. This book's journey offers hope that we find safe space and heartfelt writing that assists us finding the peace in our own heart.

Hearing the heartbeat within each of us is so powerful, because in that special space is where the fire burns. Even if one day we lose the fire, we can always rise from the ashes and reignite. We find our path as we walk alone or with someone. We get stronger along our true path, and we lift off in love as we are about to fly. We know it's our time to soar, understanding that the power we have within ourselves guides us to new heights.

# AUTHOR'S NOTE:

My heart is excited for you! And I'm glad you are holding onto this book! You might ask yourself, "Does it help me to read a book with David's stories and poems?" Yes! Because when you read some of these, you see yourself in your own experiences!

You will share in something I call *Pathfinder Perspective,* because as I read my own stories I see growth opportunities we can all see from our own experiences. We learn from the past as we live in the present. I've learned from the paths I have taken. Now I understand the right path for me to use as a runway to take off, fly true and soar. I hope the heart in this book re-ignites *your* heart to tell you, "It's Your Time To Soar!" and that we see you preparing to fly to your next level.

# THESE SPECIAL QUOTES

These two special quotes touched David Chametzky's heart early in life, and they still do.

*The most beautiful things in the world cannot be seen or even touched, they must be felt with the heart*
– Helen Keller

*The only lasting beauty is the beauty of the heart*
– Rumi

# ABOUT THE JOURNEY

## BY DAVID CHAMETZKY

We walk each other home connected by a magic thread that runs through each of our hearts. Each step along the journey is another heartbeat along our path that will eventually lead us to soar to higher places, which we have only dreamed of. We know we are alive because our hearts beat, and we feel things along the way.

I welcome you to enjoy reading and experiencing things here that might touch your heart and allow you the possibility of seeing a new path along your own journey.

Throughout the journey, our experiences are the things we cherish the most and hold dear to our own hearts. For me the journey is part personal, part spiritual, and often inspirational.

In a way, the path we choose to take in life becomes paved with heartbeats.

The beats are important, and sharing those beats allows us to sense another's beauty in many forms, building a powerful connection on a deeper level. This type of heart-felt connection holds a special alchemy — a sacred transformation in which we discover within ourselves the deeper meanings of our journey. We walk this journey together, enriching all of us, while remaining faithful to our own heart.

# HEARTBEATS

Bah Boom, Bah Boom — our first heartbeats, and our life is just beginning. These are the first sounds of life, love, and the experiences from which we learn.

With those first heartbeats the engine of our heart begins, and then, it's a continuous flood of experiences. Those include the experience we most associate with the heart — LOVE.

> The first heartbeat we hear is from our mother.
>
> Our first heartbeat's comforting rhythm sets us on our journey.
>
> Our early heartbeats give us the power of beginnings.
>
> Our heart is our center of emotion, of wisdom, of courage.
>
> Our heart is the ultimate source and symbol of love.
>
> Our heart rises with excitement and falls when we face adversary.
>
> We learn that the four chambers of our heart working in unison keeps us being well, and that our relationships working in unison bring us well being.
>
> We learn through experience that living in our head can get us into trouble, and that living in our heart is where we feed our soul.
>
> Each heartbeat can be felt differently, and each individual is unique.

# POEMS, QUOTES AND STORIES

Here is hoping that a piece of you appears as you read some of the poems, quotes and stories that follow.

## The First
*a story by David Chametzky*

That first young lady for me was Sandi. I knew her through our families and most importantly her brothers. When you are a young kid playing ball with guys it can be tough, especially on the streets of Brooklyn, New York. Not many hugs. But it's the toughness —standing up to everyone — that earns the respect, even from her brothers. Those are the ones that that eventually make you family. In Brooklyn, there are tests that "allow" you to be trusted, and when you stand up, it makes you brothers for life. Getting through the tough things we experience teaches us how to prevail and how to find plenty of smiles. I was lucky enough to find special smiles, and hugs, from Sandi. I can still see her today in my mind's eye, just as she was then.

We were both 13 (she was a few days older than me), and we created many smiles that warm my heart, even many years later. I believed then that she was too smart and beautiful to be with me, but I made her smile, and she wanted to be around me. She called me "my Goofy". We grew together and found ways to smile and enjoyed the hugs. It was then I realized hugs and smiles are unlimited.

When you are with the right person, the hugs and smiles flow so easily. We spent our middle school and high school years together. I remember that first kiss as a young teenager. I was happy just holding hands, and until that first kiss, I had never understood fully the magic I would be lucky enough to experience.

That day the sun set near the bay as we spoke about nothing much, which seemed so important to us then. I remember her blonde hair glistening and the water sparkling in the sun as I reached to her face. It was the innocent kiss of youth, and even after all these years I can remember the sweetness of her lips, and all the smiles I had walking home that afternoon.

I almost went away to college in California to be near her; however, I knew that was not the journey our relationship should take. She was going to Stanford, and I would have been satisfied just going to any college that was near her. We both felt that would be together, if we made sure our paths stayed connect.

Sandi and I shared many more smiles and positive energy over the phone during her four years at Stanford. In her senior year, she came home so we could attend a Billy Joel concert. Seeing her singing along that night jumpstarts my heart to sing with smiles, even now as I write this. It's a hug from my past. I've learned that some memories are so strong that they bring smiles just sitting in them.

My years with Sandi gave me memories of smiles and hugs to last a lifetime, including the last time I saw her. Dropping her off at the airport, I was smiling, because I knew that in a few weeks the smile on her face would be different when I asked her to marry me.

My grandfather use to say, "Men make plans, but God laughs". Being in college is stressful. Often when Sandi and I spoke, she was stressed. My take was that Sandi was perfect, and she felt the weight of the world on her shoulders. Even then I knew I couldn't change anything for her, but I knew she found peace just hearing my voice. We enjoyed talking, and I could listen to her for hours. Speaking on the phone that night I told her to go to a party and she eventually agreed. As she was walking home from the party, she was hit by a drunk driver and killed. Sandi's smile that touched my soul in so many ways would smile no longer.

To this day, when I need it the most, Sandi's smile still jumpstarts my heart. The energy of those memories of her smile still warms me. It is remarkable, and a life lesson, that I feel Sandi's positive energy, even now! That lesson from my Sandi years inspired me to become positive energy for others.

I learned the power of smiles lives on, like magic, despite the pains and challenges of life. In my life, I have hobbies and passions, like photography, to help find the magic that is waiting for us in all situations. Being a photographer you can surprise yourself at times, finding a smile or a heart in ordinary places. Our path in life bring us through many challenges, and each challenge introduces us to a new aspect of who we are, and who we are becoming – our most authentic self. Following our passions will lead to new experiences and possibilities where the magic of the smile will pop up.

Sandi was the first real love of my life. It was a gift to experience that. We don't forget the little things, which, over time, become big things that we wish for when they are gone.

## Pathfinder Perspective

What are *the firsts* you remember? A moment at the beach? Dinner with a canoe above your heads? Or a walk in a preserve, remembering your need to smile?

I shared this story to remind us all about how having that first love changes us, and it affects how we experience other relationships in our future. Looking back to my first love reminds me of the magic of love and of that first heartbeat of growth.

> **DO IT**
> BECAUSE IT'S IN YOUR
> **HEART**
> NOT BECAUSE U WANT
> SOMETHING IN RETURN

Unconditional love is given freely without any expectation of receiving anything in return. As the days in our lives come and we grow, we learn the best gift we can give is a piece of our heart with NO expectations of something in return. Sending flowers, gifts to strangers or even those we love with no expectations is our way to tell the universe we believe in love and would offer up an opportunity to others to receive it.

*Beauty is in the heart of the beholder* – H.G. Wells

# The Beginning
### a poem by David Chametzky

I remember that first kiss

The size of the moon

The taste of your lips

My heart racing as I leaned in

Your lips so soft

I held that for such a long time

How things begin and build

It all starts with the heart beats

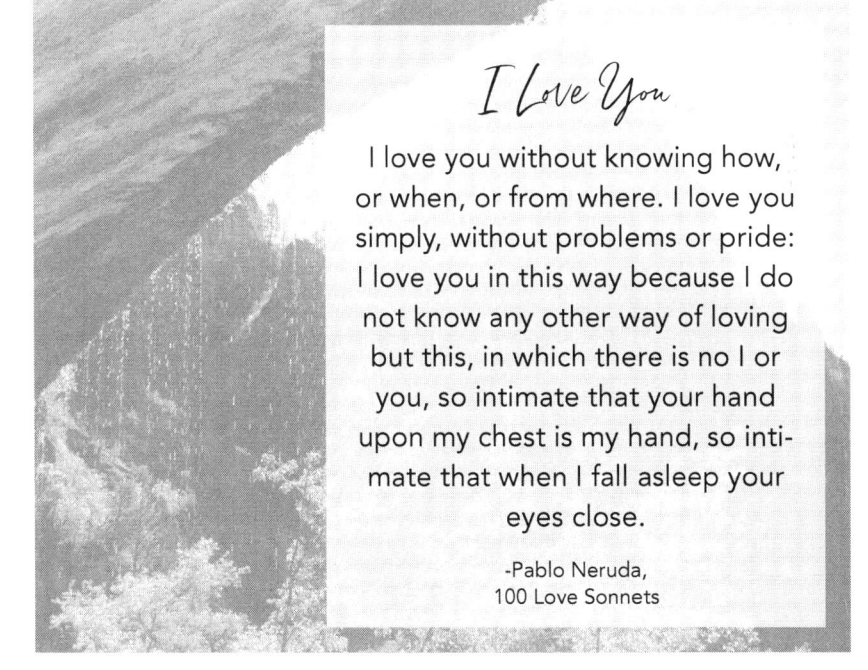

*I Love You*

I love you without knowing how, or when, or from where. I love you simply, without problems or pride: I love you in this way because I do not know any other way of loving but this, in which there is no I or you, so intimate that your hand upon my chest is my hand, so intimate that when I fall asleep your eyes close.

-Pablo Neruda,
100 Love Sonnets

# Rising Beats

a poem by David Chametzky

It beats and comes from our heart

It starts within each of us

It holds all the things that matter

The love that makes us soar

As well as the ashes that we crawl from to soar

Open up that heart when you are saddened

Open up that heart when you are happy

Its depth is endless and overflowing

"THE SECRET, ALICE, IS TO SURROUND YOURSELF WITH PEOPLE WHO MAKE YOUR HEART SMILE. IT'S THEN, ONLY THEN, THAT YOU'LL FIND WONDERLAND"

## Love Beats

a poem by David Chametzky

Whether the beat is slow or fast

Building a life from within or already here

Bah Boom Bah Boom

The beats allow the flow of love

You can still yourself

to hear them

to feel them

And the sound is Love

Love exists, shines like gold

It is shaped by each beat of our hearts

Precious and rare becoming a treasure

Cherishing the beats of your heart

*Every heart sings a song, incomplete, until another heart whispers back. Those who wish to sing always find a song. At the touch of a lover, everyone becomes a poet*
– Plato

## Peaceful silence
### a poem by David Chametzky

Vanishing inside the kisses shared

You fell asleep in my arms

Hearing the heartbeat in the silence

Listening to my own heart as it sings

Your love is so pure

Tingles up my spine

Gentle is your touch

I breathe ever so deeply as I fall asleep

Filling my mind with thoughts of you

Full is my heart when I think of you

The memory of your kisses

The touch of your skin

> "THE SECRET, ALICE,
> IS TO SURROUND
> YOURSELF WITH PEOPLE
> WHO MAKE YOUR
> HEART SMILE.
> IT'S THEN, ONLY THEN,
> THAT YOU'LL FIND
> WONDERLAND"

# Her

a poem by David Chametzky

On a summer's day long, long ago

I fell in love

So drawn to her,

That set my pulses so to race

I'll never know the how's and why's

I lost my heart to those beautiful eyes

No way to count the days and hours

And gazing into love filled eyes

A love you never need to doubt

A love I cannot live without

A love to last us all our days

The wondrous joy when you discover

That sweet surrender to your lover

A love I'll share with you always

## Always

### a poem by David Chametzky

More often than not

Words can't describe

My feelings for you

Which live deep inside

Feelings that grow stronger

With every beat of my heart

There isn't a moment

In the day where I cannot find

your face and smile

They appear in my mind

I long to be with you

And hold you so tight

To protect you and love you

Every day and each night

The moment I got there it was pitch black at Zero Dark Thirty.

As the sun began to rise you could see the fog on this cold morning.

Then the magic of the moment hit me — I looked around and saw lovers

all holding each other and just whispering as lovers can

to keep it quiet but enjoying the private moments of a new day,

a new opportunity and the start of something magical once again.

The beginning of a new day!

# Rising Warmth

### a poem by David Chametzky

I was lost alone in the darkness

You awakened with the sunrise

Over the mountains

Opened my eyes to the beauty of your heart

Finding myself with each beat

Burning away the morning fog

The feeling of connection and fire once again

Spreading as the sun rises

The light of love

Beats over the silence of darkness

Warming me like a blanket

As I close my eyes

I feel your warmth around me

I am no longer alone

*A kind heart is a fountain of gladness, making everything in its vicinity freshen into smiles*
– Washington Irving

*A loving heart is the truest wisdom*
– Charles Dickens

# Jump

### a poem by David Chametzky

Falling, falling, falling

And scared to death.

The Universe has answered my call,

And now I see you

To jump into what could be nothing

Every time I think of it,

I get so scared,

Shaking like that first moment,

That first kiss,

Our first moment together

I'm terrified

But this is what I want

And I'm so happy.

I want to jump

I'm so scared

Jump with me, hold my hand

## A Power Within

### a poem by David Chametzky

Let each wonderful beat just beat and bring the love

Hugs are unlimited and heal the heart in ways medicine cannot

A power that always sees memories

Reach always needing desires

Expanding energies of love always

Let love lift you up to soar

Soar through your heart

To your heart

*For it was not into my ear you whispered, but into my heart. It was not my lips you kissed but my soul.* – Judy Garland

*The human heart has hidden treasures, in secret kept, in silence sealed; The thoughts, the hopes, the dreams, the pleasures, whose charms were broken if revealed* – Charlotte Bronte

*You'll never find peace of mind until you listen to your heart* – George Michael

*It is only with the heart that one can see rightly; what is essential is invisible to the eye* – Antonine de Saint-Exupery

> You don't have to move
> mountains.
> Simply fall in love with
> life.
> Be a tornado of happiness,
> gratitude
> and
> acceptance.
>
> You will change the world
> just by being
> a warm, kind-hearted
> human being.

## Today and Forever

### a poem by David Chametzky

Day by day

Night by night

Kiss by kiss

Touch by touch

Step by step

I fall in love

A love so incomprehensible

So unique

A want so strong

I love you today

I'll love you tomorrow

I'll love you forever

# The Beach

a story by David Chametzky

The beach was always our little place to be – isolated from everything going on and a place where we could enjoy each other's company. It's a place where no matter what mood you were in when you got there, when you left you always felt better. It couldn't have been any better because we were together, walking along the water, waves crashing and that magical moon over our shoulders. It seems so cliché today, but it was so amazing being there then. I climbed on the rocks, and you told me to be careful. I've always felt that I couldn't get hurt when I'm with you. I danced on those rocks and could see you smile. You allowed me to be your "Goofy". We stayed at the beach to watch the sun rise. I'll never forget how, as the sun rose, it shined in your hair and made your eyes sparkle just right. I'll never forget how you looked in that moment. I don't need a picture because I'll always have one in my mind.

## Pathfinder Perspective

I have many memories of the beach as my special place which, to this day, allows me to recapture my peace. Where is your special place?

We all have that one special place within ourselves, and in a relationship, where we feel safe and connected. Today when I go to the beach alone, I often take myself back to the place where I enjoyed the beauty of those special moments.

# Rain outside Sun Inside

A poem by David Chametzky

We lie on the couch

We can hear the rain on the roof

So much to do but neither of us wanting to move

The rain was calming

I looked over to you and gave you a kiss

Your eyes widen as you lean in for another kiss

You say you love me

It was the first time in forever I heard that

I kissed you back

We just stayed there for a bit enjoying the moment

# GOOD PATHWAYS

There are many paths we take in life and some of these take us in directions that we never wanted to go. There is a saying that sometimes during the darkest times when we feel lost on our path that we find what we are looking for. Our true path is not usually one that is straight but the road that might be less traveled.

We all have been lost at times, but then out of nowhere we find a pathfinder who makes the right suggestion or helps us re-route to find magical destinations that we never would have found.

It is in those moments when we are lost that we are able to see our fears most clearly. We are also able to see our strengths, and in that moment we take the first steps in the right direction.

Walking in the Alaskan wilderness, they told us to "watch out for bears" in this section of woods. "Stay safe on the path," but the path is not always straight and it changes. We find our way through whatever life brings us.

When we become our own pathfinder and find our true path, we turn our true path into a runway from which we can take off into true flight, preparing to soar. We all learn when your heart says, "It's Your Time To Soar!"

# The Path Chosen

### a poem by David Chametzky

There are so many paths in our lives

When you find your path

You will know

Not all paths lead to love

When you find the right path

It will lead you to find your love story

There will be twists and turns

Don't allow the twists to throw you off your path

Stay true to yourself and your path

> Love is the bridge between you and everything.
> Rumi

Love is a guide

For the heart to never be lost

A beacon in the darkness

Showing the way

The paths it leads so many places

Sometimes we are never sure

Eternal and sincere

Yell from the mountaintops

Loving you is my reason

I found my path

# The Fall

    a poem by David Chametzky

Childhood memories,
the look of that someone special
passion, love, joy
they bring us so high

If that was all life
then we would not know the balance

The falls come
We have all experienced it
The lows are the opposite of the highs
Sunken with exhaustion
Clinging to kisses long lost

The fall
does not define us
How we lay in the ashes
does not define us
How the fires of life surround us
Does not define us

How we choose to get up

Building
It starts with one knee
Building
Standing shakily
Building
Small steps forward
Building

New Foundations are created
Stronger
New thought patterns
Stronger
New Points of view
Stronger

Awakened because night has fled
Risen
The suns golden light
Risen
Tree of Knowledge
Risen

Experience it all because of the fall
It does not define us
We stronger because of it
Rise once again

# The Glacier

a story by David Chametzky

There are moments in every relationship when you get clearer how you feel for another. It doesn't have to happen only once. In longer relationships it happens over and over. I've been blessed with these over-and-over opportunities. There was even one moment during a trip in which I knew in my heart that I cared more about my special someone's safety than my own.

We decided to take a trip to Iceland during one school break. Iceland in the winter is an experience I would recommend highly. The blue lagoon with the warmth of the hot springs, the steam rising into the air as it is snowing – completely a magical place. At one point the entire island was "CLOSED" because of a snowstorm which allowed us to miss sightseeing but appreciate our time together!

One of the things we did on this trip was go snowmobiling on a glacier. It let us see this whole country has a certain beauty, even with the gray skies. To get to the snowmobile you need to take a ride in a huge truck with a body 25 feet in the air that you need to climb up into. You ride in this "truck tower" looking down over the snow until you get to the glacier field where you "gear up" in the cabin for extra protection from the elements. They allow each couple to take off on one snowmobile with snow coming down and visibility not that great.

Nevertheless, off we go chasing our tour guides, going as fast as we want, and the snow keeps coming down. I am driving in the middle of the pack, constantly looking for the lights on the other snowmobiles for guidance. We go out about an hour out, trying to take in everything we can see. Frankly, feeling her arms around my waist was one of the best parts. We felt adventurous, and it was exciting! And by the time our cold fingers got to the halfway point rest stop we were both fully thrilled and ready to turn back.

We get off the snowmobiles to stretch and check in with everyone. The tour guides explain that they will give us an opportunity to "go crazy" and take some circles around this area. She asked to drive home. I immediately said, "Yes!" and then watched all the other men get on the snowmobiles. Was I disappointed? Hell No! I got to hold my love and experience the ride differently.

She gets on the snowmobile and takes off like a rocket, yelling, "Don't worry, I am just getting my bearings". I don't worry, because I get to hold her for a whole hour in an amazing place as we experience it together. She begins the circles. I sense the speed. She gets control of the vehicle. BAM! We take off like a rocket. We're making this huge turn, and the vehicle is getting faster and faster. I admit I am holding tighter now. All of a sudden we spin out of control, and the engine revs as we flip over. I'm still holding on until we spill out disoriented onto the snow. I lost hold of her for a second. I don't care about me, but where is she?

The only thought on my mind was, "What do I need to do for her?" I didn't realize the Snowmobile was on top of me and that I needed to get from under the machine which was on its side. Turns out my back was hurt, but I was uninjured, except for my pride. Most importantly, she was fine, other than being a little scared. Lying in the snow in the immediate aftermath of the accident, I only wanted to make sure she was fine. Looking through her mask and seeing her smile warmed my heart.

She kept asking in a broken voice if I was alright. I knew at that moment I needed to just pull my shit together, as the tour guides ran to us to make sure we were ok. All the other guests were looking at us – (dumb Americans) – and I could feel the other men laugh under their breath. I didn't care, because I was with my love on top of a glacier, and as we got back onto the snowmobile she held me a little tighter. While the engine raced so did my heart. I was glad she was fine, and I knew I would heal.

The sore feeling in my back did last for a few days afterwards, however, I will *never* forget the feeling of her holding me tighter on the trip back to the cabin.

## Pathfinder Perspective

While I almost got thrown off a glacier I had no regrets. In any relationship you have moments that remind you how much you love that other person and how they make you feel. [I can still remember the feeling of not knowing where she was or if she was ok. I remember seeing her smile and warming my heart.

What moments in your life might have started with worries that turned into smiles? Remember those "Soaring Heart" moments and hold onto them forever. I do.

# You

    a poem by David Chametzky

I don't think you will
ever fully understand
how you've touched my life
and made me who I am.

I don't think you could ever know
just how truly special you are
that even on the darkest nights
you are my brightest star.

I don't think you will ever fully comprehend
how you've made my dreams come true
or how you've opened my heart
to love and the wonders it can do.

You've allowed me to experience
something very hard to find
unconditional love that exists
in my body, soul, and mind.

*The only way out is through.*
— Robert Frost

# *The Magical City* – love is everywhere

**Venice is such a magical city surrounded by both new and old, traditions and history. Water, thousands of bridges and the most beautiful architecture you might see around every corner.**

When you are with the right person you will see signs of love everywhere. One of the most magical places on Earth is the city of Venice. Just hearing the name of the city brings us images of delight and dreams, even if you have not been there. It's a magical floating city over water that spreads all the way the eye can see — like a flying bird spreading its wings in all directions ready to soar.

The city is covered in water, and one sees images of shimmering lagoons, waterways filled with gondolas, palaces, church bells and intricate bridges everywhere. Among the many things the city is famous for are its blown glass, its lace, and carnival masks. The real beauty of the city is that there is romance and love at every turn.

It's also the perfect shrine of love where it can be found within each narrow street. It's a place where love reveals itself in ways you would not expect – a place lovers can renew and relish their love.

This city is an island, cut from the rest of the world with thousands of islands and water glistening like the glass made in nearby Murano. Each island sitting like a passionate lover so close to its partner but also so distant.

During one such trip to this magical city, I recall walking with my lover. We felt we had the city all to ourselves. Walking, talking and exploring in this magical place. We were passionately in love, exploring that love as we discovered the sights and tastes of Venice. During one stroll, it felt as though we were walking in a tunnel, just the two of us on a narrow street. We stopped for some gelato. Walking with ice cold gelato, our love burning between the two of us, I saw it — my most magical memory. A heavenly light transformed into a heart, reflecting from a centuries old door. "Hold my gelato!" She looked at me quizzically, trustingly. A special angle and the right lens captured that heart in our memory, forever. After the shot, I asked her if I could seal this moment with a kiss. It was more sweet than the gelato. When I showed her the photo back at the hotel I received another kiss even more sweet – further sealing the moment and magic of that day.

A heart is often found on our paths, and some paths are filled with hearts. The heart I found was as solid as the wooden door I saw it on. The thing about hearts is that they can be as colorful as all masks or as fragile as the glass in Venice. Seeing love and hearts everywhere, I felt my heart was as solid as the marble in all the palaces around us. I was a lucky man that day, and I still feel that way.

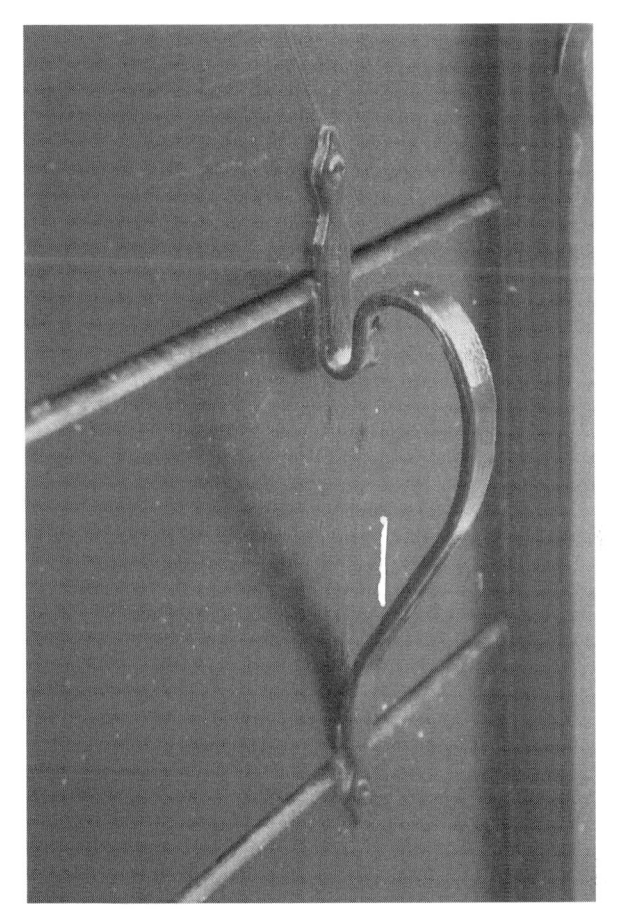

**Hearts are found everywhere**

## Pathfinders Perspective

Have you ever had that moment in life where you know it was special as it was happening?

We often find things that are special when we allow ourselves to be fully present, able to experience the magic of the moment. It does not have to be a far off location. We often only notice them when we are far off, because our senses are heightened.

My heart's wish for you is that you experience magical moments, no matter where you are.

*Wherever you go, go with all your heart*
– Confucius

# Twinkle Twinkle

a poem by David Chametzky

Your eyes sparkle as the stars in the sky

Twinkling and sparkling

Each sparkle is another memory I hope to have with you.

I look to the future both the near and the far

And see millions of memories,

Just waiting to be made.

The memories float above me,

I reach up to take some,

To catch some memories in my hands.

Let's make some memories.

Do you see them up there?

They're just waiting to happen,

These are the times we'll remember

Catch one of those stars

In our hands, minds and hearts.

# Stand By Me

### a poem by David Chametzky

Hold on

we can make it

through the storms

and the winds of change

You are not alone

On the Path

The winds could blow

we will hold each other

If the sun doesn't shine

I would still be by your side

And if the sky turns grey

We will look for the sun together

Walk this road with me

*If you carry joy in your heart
you can heal any moment*
– Carlos Santana

**The toughest paths create the strongest warriors**

Acknowledging our lives are filled with pathways & doorways,

we realize we get to choose! Do we walk in one and not another?

How important it is to choose those that keep us on our true path?

And how do we continue knowing what that path is?

Walk through the doorways and know its ok to turnaround.

# Forward through the doorway
a poem by David Chametzky

We know the doors that we want to go through

What is there on the other side

What can happen if we walk through

Fear often keeps up from walking through

While the path might not be straight

It might be full of obstacles

Our heart knows how to overcome them

Just by moving forward

The past is behind us; however, there is always a story about how our pasts create our futures.

We learn and experience from our past the lessons that we use in the future. The ruins of our past are used to build the clearer path as we move on through the portals of growth and life, towards brighter times. Use all the past as stepping stones to see clearer and higher.

## The Protector
### A poem by David Chametzky

There are things you don't know about me

Even after all these years

I'm a protector

Like they night with the kids

Someone comes in on my family

I stand between them and perceived danger

When one of my family gets attacked

I get involved no matter what

My dad was the same way

You don't know the past few months

I would cry myself to sleep

Something wasn't right with us

My dad had just passed

My mom moved.

Teenage girls are an experience

You are my constant

Tears of joy for you.

I don't share because you seem distant

One of our girls asked me if you are ok

I tried to talk to you

## Good Pathways

I love you and always will.

Our paths got crossed and I am lost

I will find my way

Up the hills and down the valleys

Finding the right path

Some paths are rocky and others are smooth and straight. There are those of us who might want to only walk on the easy path. The real test for us is how we walk on the tougher paths. Even though it is rocky and winding there are lessons to be learned. There is some adventure and excitement. We learn how to keep walking, finding the balance required, and knowing the true path. The true path will take you exactly where it is supposed to take you. You might not always end up where you want to be, but you will end up where you need to be.

# *Resolute* – inner heart will win the battle

a story by David Chametzky

The heart knows what it wants. The strong willed do not give up until they get what they want to achieve. I went to Yosemite National Park, because I wanted to get away from so many things, and I knew if I submersed myself in nature I would heal in ways I would never be able to do in the city. The power of reconnecting ourselves to nature and mother earth is amazing. Being in nature allows each of us to tap into our innate ability to renew our own hearts.

On this trip I brought my best friend, because he was always up for traveling. I had many memories of things that had occurred on our trips, but this trip was special. Although I was more fit physically, Kevin wouldn't let things set him back just because of his ailments. He was determined to see the beauty of Yosemite. As we drove out of San Francisco, he reminded me, at what seemed like every mile marker, that he wasn't sure how much hiking he was going to be able do. For those of you who never drove to Yosemite there is a road with thousands of turns and switchbacks as you climb to the top of Yosemite Valley. We laughed and joked a lot, even when he got car sick.

One cannot experience *all* the beauty of Yosemite in just one short visit, but we did our best. As we planned out the "must see" places, we decided to take the hike up to Vernal Falls and further up to Nevada Falls. For those not familiar with this particular hike, it's a 5-mile round trip. That doesn't sound bad – but this hike is known for being strenuous, and dangerous. But hey, you get to see two amazing waterfalls as well as a mist bath. Even Kevin was determined to make the effort!

The path starts off paved, offering beautiful views and luring us into the real physical test — soon the path turns into an uphill ascent, gradual at first and steeper by the footstep. I looked over at Kevin, and he was already struggling. I checked on him and told him about all the views that we were going to see. He took his time and kept looking at the squirrels until we came upon an encouraging sign: "650 steps to Vernal Falls". I looked over at Kevin. He took a deep breath and said, "Let's Go!" Even though he was struggling with his legs *and* his asthma, he knew he was 650 steps from reaching the top of Vernal Falls. I could tell he was giving himself a little silent pep talk. It was exciting, because we could hear the roar of the falls, and Kevin kept saying he wanted to see that. It was a test he wanted to pass for himself.

The amusing thing about the personal tests we give ourselves is that those who aren't successful often don't take the steps necessary to reach what their heart wants. In contrast, there are people who have been told their entire lives, "You can't", then, when faced with a moment of challenge or opportunity, their heart chooses to push further than ever before.

With Kevin's determination, we both made it to Vernal Falls and the roaring of the water. Then there was an even steeper climb, if we were going to make Nevada Falls. The trip so far had taken much longer than we had expected, and I could see that Kevin's ailments were draining him. At least we'd made it to Vernal Falls, and the view was truly gorgeous. As we rested, I didn't think he could go on. Then he looked over to me and said, "Let's Go! We have another one to climb!"

As steep as the climb up to Vernal Falls was — the next part got more difficult. It's a lot more uphill walking, and it lulls you in with the Emerald Pool — a shallow lake with bright emerald colored water. Right after the pool, the near vertical stairs begin across a granite mountain. The beauty draws you in as each step gets you closer. I check on Kevin and he is slowly pushing through. As we get closer, the phrase "So close, yet so far" comes into my head. I am watching someone who is more challenged physically preserve his energy, because he wanted this test of his heart. He wanted to see the top of this particular mountain.

It was not easy climbing over these granite stairs, with each step feeling the burn in my legs. I looked back and could see the determination in him. The funny thing is, this hike, while strenuous for Kevin, was really a test for *both* of us. We both could have stopped, and no one but us would have known. The tempting mist of the waterfalls reminded us we were here to get to the top. I learned later on exactly how much it meant to Kevin.

We can be proud of ourselves when we accomplish things that no one thought possible (sometimes even ourselves). As we reached the top of Nevada Falls the sun was shining, and the smile of my friend was even brighter. He didn't want to call his girlfriend, he wanted to personally enjoy being at the top of *his* mountain. His body had been climbing with all the physical strength he could muster. Now his heart was soaring like an eagle. -

Kevin was with me on many more trips. No matter where we traveled, anytime I mentioned Nevada Falls, his beaming smile reflected that day when his body persevered and his heart soared.

## **Pathfinders Perspective:**

What have you done that you knew you needed to accomplish?

What "mountain" have you climbed no matter what?

How did that feel?

While many of the poems and stories in this book are romantic in nature, that is not the only thing our hearts are for. Hearts test a person, and at times we do rise from our ashes, and we even end up soaring in places we didn't know we were able to reach. Kevin was my best friend, and he took this trip to help *me* through some challenging times after my divorce. Not only did he give all his heart to people, it was my honor to share some very magical moments with him (even when he complained about my snoring). He was always there for me and I was blessed to get the opportunity to be there for him in a big way.

Who is your Kevin? Do you let them know? Whose Kevin are you?

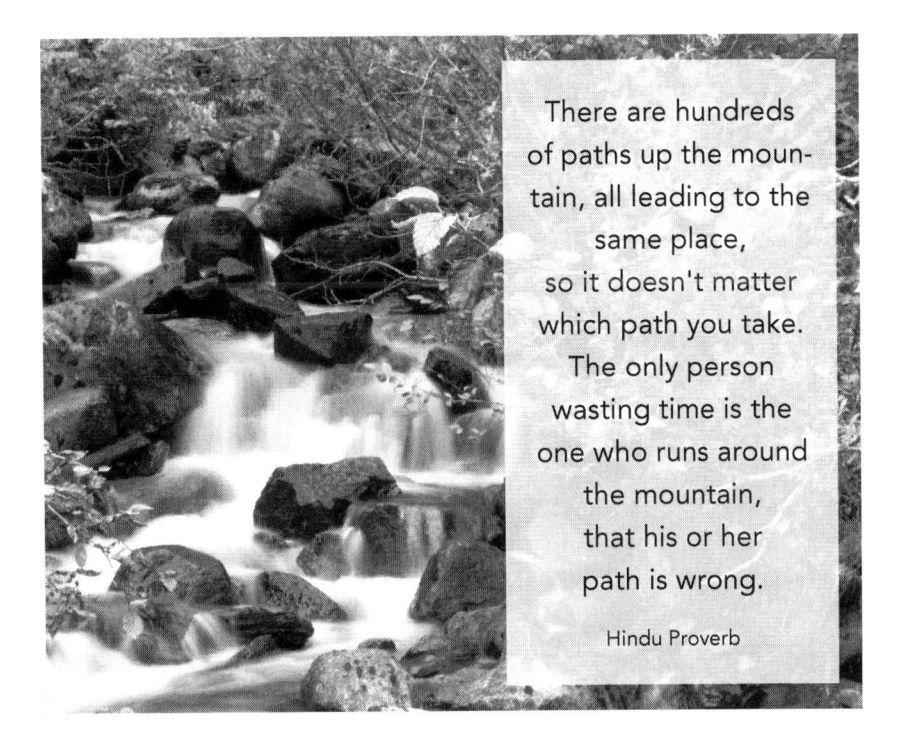

> There are hundreds of paths up the mountain, all leading to the same place, so it doesn't matter which path you take. The only person wasting time is the one who runs around the mountain, that his or her path is wrong.
>
> Hindu Proverb

*Put your heart, mind, and soul into even your smallest acts. This is the secret of success*
— Swami Sivananda

*Son, brother, father, lover, friend. There is room in the heart for all the affections, as there is room in the heaven for all the stars*
— Victor Hugo

*Love the life you live. Lead the life you love.*
— Bob Marley

# TRUE FLIGHTS

**It is your time to soar!** In the beginning we heard our heart beat and learned to grow. Then as we took our steps we walked on our path and sometimes got lost until we found the right path. Once on the right path we learned that it takes strength and speed to go faster and further than we could ever have imagined. When we gain the speed and confidence then we are ready to soar. Now it's time to soar either for our first time or to the next levels of our life's journey.

Soaring we sometimes find turbulence but still want to reach higher. We can soar above the storms or just ride the winds to find calmer skies. In doing so we experience many things and can even find our way through those storms and end up right where we need to be.

# True Flights

Sometimes we are in the garden of our life.

It's the place we didn't know we need to be.

We wait for the right moment for everything.

Sometimes it doesn't happen. Sometimes it does!

Waiting for the right moment of beauty,

the caterpillar becomes the butterfly.

Those right moments are fleeting,

but they live long in our hearts.

If we don't stay open and look for the beauty and love in the moment we can easily miss those right moments.

If we stay open, we can cherish them for a lifetime.

## Standing tall and seeing the light that guides us all

One of my first times at the lighthouse, I was there with my love showing her the world through my eyes. I use my camera to show her how I see things from other perspectives. She smiled.

Some of the perspectives were simple, and I could see the smile I would fall in love with. Looking up, we saw the glow of the sun and the day before us reflecting on all and lighting our path. Seeing our true path before me that day, I was compelled to follow her radiant smile into the beautiful skies of our future together.

# Guided by the Light
### a poem by David Chametzky

There is one great treasure that shines day and night,

Love

It is the light house in the storm of life

The storms and tides,

to which my ship looks for

Always looking for the safe light of love

Trusting and hoping to see the light.

Love will guide me through the storm

Your touch has rescued me

from the rough seas

You held me through the storm

**I feel safe in your arms**

## Fireworks

a poem by David Chametzky

The wind flew through your hair as the sun set

Your face glows in the setting sun

All I wanted was a kiss

Sweetness as our lips touch

I feel your lips on mine

Fireworks explode in my body

Bright flashes of light;

Then spider webs of color.

The night sky lights up

Splashes of color in the dark,

Flowers in the night,

Blooming amidst the stars.

Stars of rainbow colors,

I am holding you

Soaring with the Fireworks

All is beautiful

LOVE

# Into the stars
## a poem by David Chametzky

I lie on the ground,

and stare into space,

the stars start to move,

into the shape of your face.

I see you there now,

looking down at me,

with that cute little smile,

that I like to see.

Soaring to kiss you .

## Soaring Warrior

a poem by David Chametzky

Firm in her faith

Courageous, strong, loving

self-assurance

Eyes aglow with life

Smile as strong as the sun

Inner energy more powerful than can be imagined

Scars both seen and unseen

Strength tapped from all resources

Incredible energy generated

A warrior lives within

Filled with pearls

Wisdom, Joys

Opportunities expanding

Scary but forward always

Staying strong from the heart

Love is offered

Shields are strong

Brave is the option

That is what a warrior does.

# Storms

a poem by David Chametzky

Life is like a ship in a storm

Imagine a ship sailing the sea

Everything is great in calm seas

The rough seas shows the character of the ship

the years go by and the ship endures

storms hit that ship so hard some days

Love is what keeps it sailing during the storm

Sometimes nothing but love keeps it sailing

even when it was tough

Love held on to that ship

day after night

Love is the lifeboat in the storms of life.

I hope we ride out the storms together

# Ancestral Guide

### a poem by David Chametzky

"My child you've been through so much

And through it all you've stood.

It is not your time

You have work to do

A hand was held out

So I could be led

When I was going to ask

How a loving God could let me bleed,

He stepped aside to show me.

Showed me what I already knew

The answers are inside

I will use my experience

To guide others through the storm.

Find clearer skies

seeing further than one can imagine

Soaring even when your feet are on the ground.

# The Light

a poem by David Chametzky

As the stars shine in the darkness of the night

your eyes fill the sky and turn the dark in to light

your smile are the suns rays

your laughter powers the sea.

Brightness that can be blinding

You're everything I have wished for,

I'm ecstatic that you have let me in

If love is what makes the world go round

Then round and round I want to go with you

*Happiness I firmly believe that any man's finest hour, the greatest fulfillment of all that he holds dear, is the moment when he has worked his heart out in a good cause and lies exhausted on the field of battle*
– Vince Lombardi

# Angel Found

### a poem by David Chametzky

There once was a sad boy

the boy wanted to be happy

He dreamed of beautiful angels

He read a story about one angel

This angel seemed to make his heart jump

And his heart jumped with joy

Could he meet this angel

would he actually talk to the angel

The thought of it all scared him

Fate stepped in and the boy jumped at the chance

The boy met the angel

The angel was full of love and life

The angel is everything his heart wished for

Sometimes wishes do get fulfilled

The boy became a man again

Thank you my angel

*Love is of all passions the strongest, for it attacks simultaneously the head, the heart and the senses.*
– Lao Tzu

# Forever

a poem by David Chametzky

I think of you so often you have no idea

I don't think you could ever feel

All the love I have to make available to you

You've made my dreams come true

Opened my heart and filled it with memories of a lifetime

No matter what I will never stop loving you.

*A Gentle heart is tied with an easy thread*
– George Herbert

# Universal Connections

a poem by David Chametzky

I carry your heart with me

It is never far from me.

Here is the deepest secret nobody knows

Life; which grows higher than soul can hope

This is the wonder that's keeping the stars apart

Once in every lifetime, someone comes along,

The one special heart

You've been waiting for your whole life long.

Once in every lifetime, God sends an angel from above,

To make your life complete

Who you can give your endless love.

When a love like this comes, make any sacrifice,

For the best things in life

To fly among the stars and with angels to be with you.

## Perfect Souvenir –
a trip cementing memories in my heart.

While there are so many unknowns on our journey, the one constant is that the sun is brighter with you in my life! We can choose to be a rock for ourselves and for others – a firm foundation, something to lean on to keep you upright. It is a choice, and we chose each other — newly engaged!

When we stand together we become bigger than just ourselves.

# The Souvenir

a story by David Chametzky

When you go on a trip you hope to come home with memories, experiences and sometimes the perfect souvenir. I remember the planning of this trip. Every time there was that glimmer in her eye that brought me to a special place I have always loved. It was the light that let me see into her eyes and soul. So many times, I had a glimpse of it, and at that moment I would do anything to see and experience that special spark within her — she had an energy and power from within that recharged my soul. For me it was like being around the sun. It was bright and warm and you can feel recharged just being her presence.

There are moments during the planning and even the trip I took "pictures" in my mind of the things I wanted in my heart. She had already owned mine, and I wanted to build castles of love for her that would last thousands of years like the ones were about to see.

As we board the plane I look at you and smile. We get to our seats and looking into your eyes I see that sparkle and I reach in for a kiss. So soft but also so deep. I just keep thinking of how amazing you are and how lucky I am with you in my life. I remember looking over at you as you closed your eyes resting. In my eyes, you are an angel. You shine in so many ways.

This trip starts off right with some museums and even a beer factory tour. We had lots of laughs, especially during our dinner tour of the city that included Domino's Pizza and ice cream delivered to our tour boat. How you smile about simple things is one of your precious traits in my eyes. We enjoy our time together, and whatever we see is perfect. Being together is *the most* important thing, and it brings me great joy as we walk around one of the world's most magical cities. We heard people aboard a floatilla of boats singing "You've Got a Friend". We marveled at street performers galore, sensed magic everywhere, and experienced some of the most amazing things that the world has to offer, and *none* of it mattered as much as having you right next to me.

I learn so much from this trip about the depth you have as a person, and about how deeply I am in love with you. You are a diamond, and I learn how brightly you shine. You're quiet, reserved and full of life, and there is so much more. I feel lucky to be finding how deep you are.

It is a perfect Sunday as we ride our bikes — July 4th in America, but we're not in America. It is ironic in some ways that we are celebrating America's independence in a country that helped fund some of it. As we walk to the bike shop, I keep thinking of how much I am in love with you. You smile and I want to keep telling you how much I love you and how I want to be with you the rest of my life. We eventually get on the bikes and ride through this magical city out into the beautiful country side.

During our bike ride in Amsterdam under the windmills with the ducks quacking, I almost ask you to marry me right there with the ducks. I will admit the thought of riding a bicycle did not excite me at first. However, it did excite you, and if it excited you, then I was all for it. This bike trip is amazing and is more than what I could have expected. I see how you're beautiful inside and out, and I want you in my life.

Our stops along this trip included Paris and all the beauty of that city. Seeing the Eiffel Tower, The Louvre, Mount St. Michel, Versailles, is so powerful, but it is our moments in Monet's Gardens at Giverny that I think of most often. I am getting 'museumed out' when you find a tour that lets us see both Versailles and Monet's Gardens! Wow! Again that magic in trusting you brings me more rewards than I could have imagined. You are amazing.

Walking in Monet's Gardens is like another dream, and you allow me the time to see and experience something that I'll never forget. The photograph I captured of the orange butterfly on the on the yellow flower symbolizes so much of who you are. A butterfly does not know how beautiful it is – it just flies around and everyone enjoys appreciating the colors as they float in the air. In the garden there are colors and beauty all around, and the beauty I keep noticing is you. I capture the photo in my mind's eye as you walk across the bridge above Monet's waterlily ponds.

The moments with you fly by, because I soar best when I am around you. Our next stop brings us to London — a city filled with the most amazing objects that the world has to offer. The two "heart memories" I have are our ice cream moment in Harrod's department store and the sun shining behind you as you said, "If you ask me to marry you I might say yes." We hadn't yet talked about marriage. My heart leapt just knowing that you were feeling what I felt.

That next morning, we rise early for our special trip to Stonehenge to see the sun rise. You sleep in the car on my shoulder as I held you. Watching you sleep so peacefully I know what I want — the trip to never end.

Arriving at Stonehenge, I take a mental inventory of everything around us. The damp fog rising from the wet grass, the wooly sheep making their welcoming "Baahs", the crisp smell of the air, and your warm hand holding mine as we walk from the parking lot to the mystical stones. As the sun rises the light glistens in your eyes as we walk around investigating, taking in the moments. I don't want to allow the moments to fleet away, I want to take each one in, especially the moment I am about to create.

I walk over to you and ask you to look around at the stones. We don't know how they got there, and there is a power you can feel being among them. I look into your eyes and say that these stones are like my love for you, that they always stand tall and will never waver or be chipped away. At that moment I ask you to marry me, offering you the ring I have carried the entire trip, awaiting this moment. "Would you give me the honor to have you and your girls enter into my heart?" At that moment I hear my heart beats.

I still feel what I felt that day – your "YES!" is my perfect souvenir!

## Pathfinders Perspective

Have you ever resisted doing something, then later, you cherished having done it?

Have you experienced something that engaged every one of your senses?

Have you ever experienced a magical moment that other people just couldn't understand?

People have told me that Stonehenge is not a romantic place. On the contrary, I found the love energy among those mystical stones. Our vacation and its final day at Stonehenge was one of the most magical chapters of my life.

*Prayer is not asking. It is a longing of the soul. It is daily admission of one's weakness. It is better in prayer to have a heart without words than words without a heart* – Mahatma Gandhi

Soaring Higher and higher above the clouds of our life.

# Roaring Higher

a poem by David Chametzky

The ocean roars

What does it say

I sit watching the waves crash

I sit and am mesmerized

It is whispering to me

Speak from your heart

Open your heart it says

The waves dance

Of loves lost and found

Hold on tight

There is magic for me in the letter "R". I always emphasize that there is an "R" within our hearts. It is amusing to me that the words Heart and Earth share the same letters. When I think of "R", I think of the power of Resilience which allows a person to Rise. I think of your love Radiating warmth like the sun and how the Remembrance of your love Renew my smiles, Rejuvenating my spirit and Re-Igniting my desire to Reach and bring value to the lives of others.

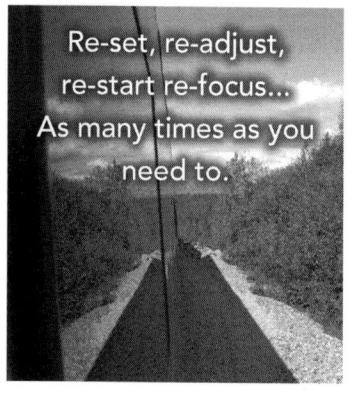

> Re-set, re-adjust, re-start re-focus... As many times as you need to.

## Being Out Of My Mind In Love

a story by David Chametzky

Let's talk about being in love. Sometimes we can't explain everything that goes on in life. We know what feels good and what does not. When you love someone you sometimes do things that seem very natural to you and that make others think you have lost your senses. Let's just say that the gift of unconditional love is one of the most special gifts we can give or receive in our life. We use that gift in many ways including lifting up another person, or soothing another person's pain or loss.

It was a Wednesday in the middle of April. I had just gotten off the phone with you and was still adjusting to your being at college on the other side of the country. It was rough. You called me as usual. You knew that you could count on me to lean on. We always leaned on each other when we needed someone to cheer us up, to brighten our day. While we only talked for a few minutes, I could see your smile in my mind's eye, and I knew that somehow I had cheered you up.

Later that day I called you back. Months had passed, and it was easy to feel empty. Not seeing you for months was really killing me. I needed to see you. Your roommate picked up the phone and said that you had gone out jogging after I had cheered you up. It was right then that I decided I would dance that fine line of out-of-my-mind love versus practical logic. I decided to use my new credit card to fly across the country and surprise you.

The first thing that I had to figure out was how was I going to get away with this without my parents knowing. I must have done a good job covering my tracks, because parents never knew about this trip, or at least never let on. What was I thinking? Buying a plane ticket on credit? Flying all the way across the country to a city where I knew only one person—you? How was I going to pull this off? When you are in love you find ways. Ways to do what your heart wants to do. I found, or created, the solutions I needed, and I did not share this with anyone. Why? I did not want anyone to talk me out of this!

After working out my cover, I made the call. The airlines were happy to oblige me as I used my new credit card. After all the arrangements were set, I called back your roommate so she could help me know where you would be when I arrived. The plans were set for me to fly out early Saturday morning and fly back Sunday evening. It was going to be one expensive night, but seeing you made it all worth it.

I was so excited. In the next two days I was waiting for something to go wrong. I was delighted when everything worked out as planned. Friday night I didn't sleep too well, I was so excited and scared. My alarm clock rang and I jumped out of bed and I was raring to go. I ran out of the house before anyone realized that I was gone.

I got to the airport and onto the plane. I wanted to scream in delight, because I had made it! We stopped in Kansas City for fuel and additional passengers. As you might expect, someone finally sat next to me. It was a woman in her early sixties. I must have looked friendly, because she started talking to me right away. When I told her what I was doing, she told me that it was the most romantic thing that she had ever heard of! By the time the plane landed I was ready to jump out of the plane. I don't know if it was from excitement or to get away from this woman. She was sweet, but all I wanted was to be left alone and to think about seeing you in person.

I ran down the runway to see your roommate. I got to the end of the tunnel and I saw your roommate smiling. Then that woman who would not stop talking on the plane walked up to your roommate and told her how lucky she was to have such a wonderful boyfriend. We smiled and she moved on, thank goodness.

I knew part of the plans were for you friends to take you out for the afternoon and that they would call later to see if I had arrived. I knew that the roses I had sent you earlier that morning were received. Your roommate also told me you had tried to call me to thank me for the roses, but I wasn't home – I was probably somewhere closer to you than you ever could have realized. I was so excited that I was moments away from seeing you!

As we were leaving the airport I bought you more flowers. I grabbed the flowers and ran to your room. In your room I waited for the phone call from your friends to tell me that you would be arriving soon. Finally, after what seemed like forever the phone rang. It was the call I was waiting for.

I didn't know what to do while I was waiting. I decided to put the second set of flowers in a place that you would see the flowers immediately when you walked in. As I heard the key go in the lock, my heart raced. You opened the door and saw the second set of flowers and I saw you start to smile. I then said "Would you like to tip the delivery man?" The look on your face was worth everything. Stunned, you jumped into my arms. I grabbed you and we fell on your bed. I won't ever forget the look on your face or the feeling of you in my arms. It was the best feeling in the world. You kept smiling and saying that you couldn't believe what I had done.

We talked for hours before anyone interrupted us. Then you insisted on introducing me to all of your friends. I loved it only because I saw how happy you were to be with me again. After not seeing each other for so long, I was wondering if things would be the same between us. After seeing your reaction, I knew that nothing would ever change between us.

We spent the rest of the day enjoying being together. Being together was so special! You took me to the beach, and we watched the sun go down near Fisherman's Wharf. As night fell, we went back to your room. We were both tired but we stayed up the whole night. I know that we both did fall asleep because I had woken up just to look at you sleeping. It seemed as though you were still glowing. You looked so comfortable.

In the morning you cooked me breakfast. You had made me breakfast before, but I think this was the best breakfast that I ever ate. It was probably the company that made it so special. Soon after breakfast it was time for me to get ready to leave. I didn't want to leave you, but I knew that I had to.

When I arrived home, your brother picked me up at the airport. He said he couldn't believe I actually did it. Of course, I never did anything like this again. Sometimes I think about this trip and that day that we spent together. Whenever I do think about it, I smile. It must have been love that made me do something like this, that many people would think was crazy. I didn't care because it made you smile, and that was all I ever wanted.

## Pathfinders Perspective

What have you done to surprise a loved one?

Did you ever do something that was irrational in the name of love? Would you do it again?

Love makes us do strange things. You can see from my story that I have done things many people would consider crazy. I am certainly guilty of honoring the people whom I love, and I have felt supported in many ways that are *not coincidence*. One example was the time I ordered one bouquet of flowers from a nationally recognized provider. The bouquet was delivered, and I got an email confirmation. However, it was not the bouquet that I ordered. It was for Mother's Day and I wanted the person to receive what I ordered. I called customer service and told them of the mistake.

They apologized and promised a correct bouquet would be delivered and I thanked them. When the delivery came, Customer Service called me, and I thanked them again, but I pointed out the order was still incorrect explaining it was ok if they did not send a third set of flowers. This went on for one month and four (4) bouquets. They finally got it right. I don't know what happened, but I do know I had dreams about the original set of flowers and vase the entire month, and I heard a voice finally saying, "I got it". Sometimes we must let the universe take charge and enjoy the ride.

# The Hug

### A poem by David Chametzky

You sometimes don't know what you need

Being strong

It is so difficult holding it all together

Having some look at you in times of distress

I held it all together until that moment

Grabbed into a hug

A hug I never knew I needed

I released it all and hugged back

It all came out of me

The weight and enormity of the situation

The hug that healed

ALWAYS A "R" IN HEART THERE IS **RISE** ALWAYS A "R" IN HEART THERE IS

**PEACE LOVE AND BRING A BAT**

# My R is always in my Heart
### a poem by David Chametzky

Ruminating how much you radiate like the sun

Refreshing as the flowing springs

Creating a love so ravenous that I would do anything for you

Knowing that at one time you reciprocated your love for me

That first kiss and the recoil but then reaching in once again

I look forward to always be rejuvenated when I am around you.

My love is relentless for you and only wants to see your happiness

Reminiscent of the times we spent together

Knowing my love is resolute for you

## A Kiss that makes you soar

a poem by David Chametzky

A kiss is all I asked for

Your heart is what I have been given

I embrace the feelings

Something is taking place

Fate has us in its arms

My fate was sealing with the first kiss

Cemented by the touch of your skin on mine

Whispers of love in your ear

Feelings so strong

# Soaring Heart

a poem by David Chametzky

I offer you my Heart

If I could go back in time

Lifting the veil

letting you see the love I have for you

Years of being held back

Letting go of the boundaries

Freely allowing myself to soar

Do you know what happens to a Soaring Heart?

Feel fully the love felt or experienced

My heart lightens up just with the thought of you

Soaring in the love of your embrace

# Generations

a poem by David Chametzky

Saying I love you is one thing – living I love you is a whole other story

Suddenly all my ancestors are behind me.

I need to still my heart I hear the words

"Watch and Listen – you are the result of the love of thousands"

We can change generations in front of us

We can heal generations behind us

Live with the generations before us

Love never ends

**The first heartbeat we hear is our mothers.**

As I put the final touches on this book, my own mother leaves her own final touches on my heart during her journey on earth. I am blessed to have been able to say everything I needed to say, apologize for all the things I needed to apologize for, and be held one more time by my mother. As my hand held hers for one of the final times, she rubbed my hand trying to still take care of me. While we might never know when our end will be, we can make sure that our hearts are filled with love, memories and the knowledge that unconditional love is the most special feeling a human can have. Even during our most sad times we can chose to flip the energy to allow more love in and remember that Love Never Ends.

During the writing of this book my mother gained her wings with a heart that I heard from the inside. She allowed me to journey on my path and yes even get lost but with the knowledge that I would be loved without a doubt. Eventually with that knowledge I learned to rise from my ashes and soar to new heights.

# AMPLIFLUENCE
## AMPLIFY YOUR INFLUENCE

## You're the Expert, but are you struggling to Monetize your Authority?

### Amplify Your Influence in 3 Sessions

**Speak Your Message**

**Publish Your Message**

**Convert Your Message**

**Check Out All Of Our 'Live' Tour Stops**

Authors and Speakers often find themselves struggling to build a strategy that actually makes them money.

amplifluence.com

SCAN FOR TOUR INFO

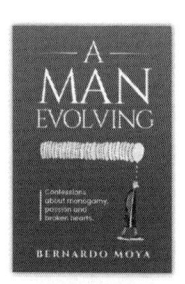

More Books From **Perfect Publishing**

www.PerfectPublishing.com

More Books From **Perfect Publishing**

www.PerfectPublishing.com

Made in the USA
Columbia, SC
17 February 2023